GEOMETRY EVERYWHERE!

VISTA®
HIGHER LEARNING

Boston, Massachusetts

MATH

Right angles, triangles . . . lines, areas, and formulas! Do we really need **geometry**? It's all just for math tests, right? Absolutely not!

Look around! Geometry is everywhere. People use it at home, at work, and at play. You can use it in your daily life, too. Let's find out how!

KNOW IT ALL

The word *geometry* comes from Greek. The word *geo* means "Earth" and *metria* means "measurement."

Let's say that you want to change the color of your bedroom. How much paint do you need? You can use a geometric **formula** to find the **area** of your walls. Find the **length** and **height** of the walls. Multiply. Subtract the area of the windows and doors. Then, **calculate** how much paint you need.

A one-gallon can covers up to 400 square feet. Will one can be enough for your room?

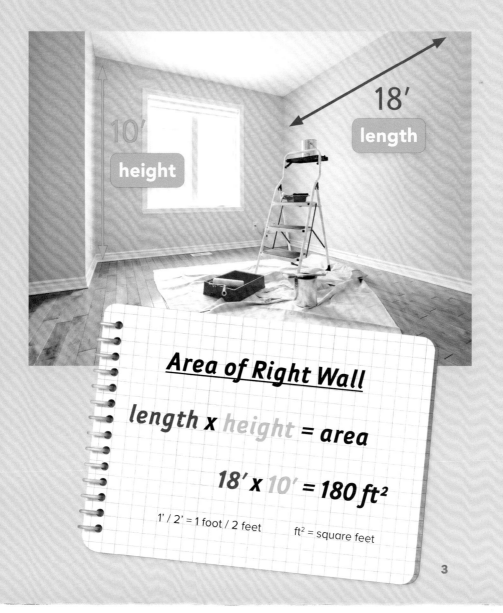

18'
length

10'
height

Area of Right Wall

length x height = area

18' x 10' = 180 ft²

1' / 2' = 1 foot / 2 feet   ft² = square feet

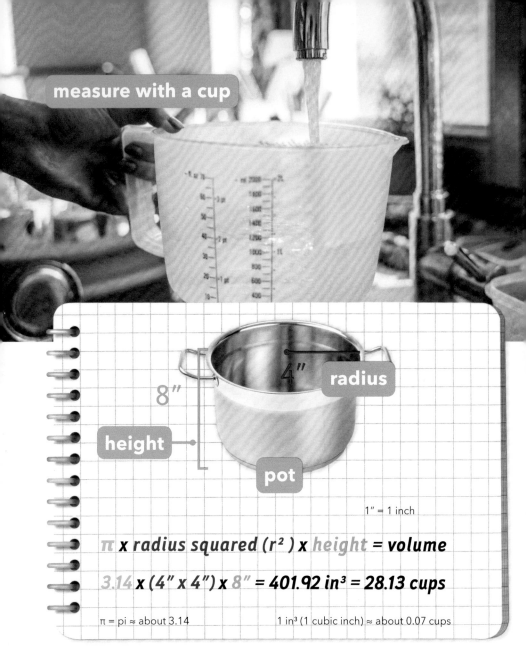

measure with a cup

8"

height

4"

radius

pot

1" = 1 inch

π x radius squared (r²) x height = volume

3.14 x (4" x 4") x 8" = 401.92 in³ = 28.13 cups

π = pi ≈ about 3.14   1 in³ (1 cubic inch) ≈ about 0.07 cups

Here's another example. You're having a party and you want to make soup for a large group of friends. You need *a lot* of soup! Which pot is going to be big enough? You can **measure** the **volume** of each pot one cup at a time. Or you can use a formula to calculate the volumes. It's much easier!

Let's take geometry outside of the house now. Imagine that you want to make a garden. How big will it be? What shape will it have? What will you need to make it? Find the area and make a plan.

Do you want a border around the garden? How many border pieces will you need? Measure the length and **width** of the garden. Multiply both by two to find the **perimeter**. That tells you the length of your border.

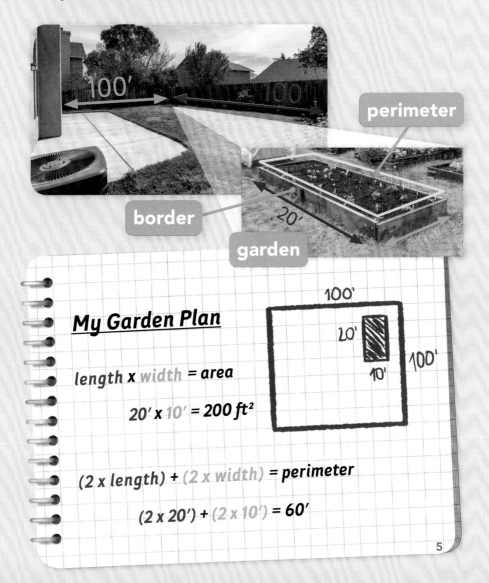

My Garden Plan

length x width = area

$20' \times 10' = 200\ ft^2$

(2 x length) + (2 x width) = perimeter

(2 x 20') + (2 x 10') = 60'

It's time for art class. Do you need geometry for art, too? Of course you do! The world is made up of shapes. So, you also use shapes when you draw pictures. Do you want to make the buildings in your picture look more real? Use different **angles**. Measure them. Add shadows. There! Now your picture looks **3-D**!

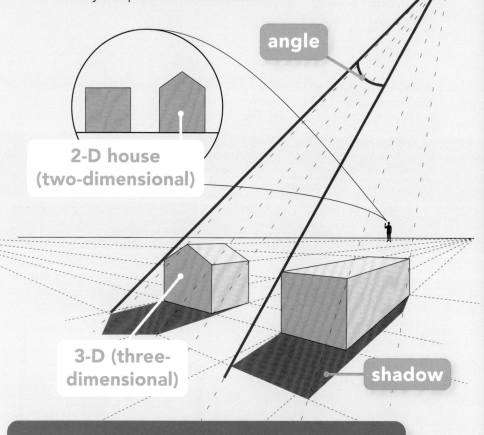

angle

2-D house
(two-dimensional)

3-D (three-
dimensional)

shadow

KNOW IT ALL

Drawings are really 2-D, but you can add different lines and angles. This makes it look like you're viewing the object from a certain point. It adds height, width, and **depth**. Drawing objects to look 3-D is called *perspective drawing*.

All artists use geometry. Some artists use repeating shapes to make **patterns**.

pattern

Other artists use shapes in interesting ways.

Some art looks more real, but if you look, you can see lines and shapes. You can see angles and shadows. Geometry is in there!

artist

There is even geometry in our clothes. For example, lots of fabrics that we wear have patterns on them.

fabric

People also make clothes using geometry. They measure fabric and cut shapes. They sew along straight lines as well as around angles and circles.

You can also see geometry in many other things that we use every day.

screen

animated movie

People use geometry to make the pictures in video games, too. In fact, some games are all about shapes! But geometry can help make anything on the screen look 3-D.

It works the same for artists who make cartoons and animated movies. They use shapes and angles to make the pictures look 3-D.

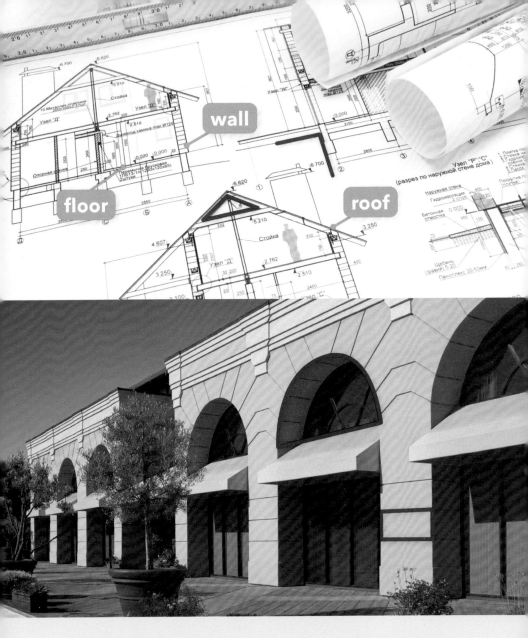

Geometry is certainly needed for building things. Engineers use it to make plans for houses, schools, offices, and other kinds of buildings. Workers use it when they measure, cut, and put together floors, walls, and roofs. Buildings won't stand without the right geometry. Your house is safe because of geometry!

People use geometry to build important things in our communities, such as bridges and streets. They use it to make the furniture we use inside our homes and offices, too.

People have been using geometry to build things for thousands of years. If you look, you can find shapes in everything. You'll see triangles, rectangles, ovals, and circles. You'll see pyramids, **cylinders**, and **spheres**!

pyramids

How about you? Do you want to build something? You'll probably need geometry!

KNOW IT ALL

Euclid *(yew-klid)* was a Greek mathematician He is known as the father of geometry. He put together some very important books on geometry around 300 BCE. He based much of his work on others. He studied the work of earlier Greek mathematicians.

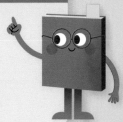

Most hockey rinks are the same size. They're the same length. They're the same width.

distance

hockey rink

Geometry is even important in sports! For example, look at this hockey rink. Most hockey rinks are the same size. Do you see the shapes and lines inside the rink? They're usually in the same place and at the same distance from each other. This helps to keep the game fair.

hockey stick

puck

Look at the hockey stick. See the angle at the end? It's perfect for players to hold it on the ice and hit the puck with it. Now look at the puck. What shape is it? Is it a sphere? No, it's flat. . . . Maybe it's a circle? Wait, a circle is 2-D, but this is 3-D. It's a short cylinder!

Players use geometry in the game, too. Before they hit the puck, they think about angles and distances. They need to calculate quickly!

Nature is full of geometry! You can find shapes and patterns in plants and trees, as well as in things that animals make.

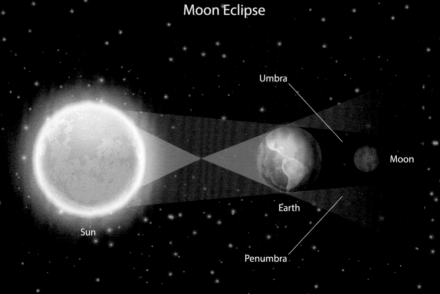

Moon Eclipse

Umbra

Moon

Earth

Sun

Penumbra

You can even find geometry in the sky. Did you know that scientists use geometry to study space? It helps them measure and calculate things like size and distance.

So, you see? Geometry isn't just for math class or tests. It's everywhere around us. It's part of our lives, whether we realize it or not. This makes it important to learn more about it. Make geometry a part of your life. You never know when you might need it!

geometry the area of math that studies points, lines, angles, and shapes

formula a rule that uses letters and numbers to show something in math or science

area the amount of space occupied by a flat (2-D) shape

length the measurement of the longest side or from one end to another

height how tall or short something is or the measurement from top to bottom

calculate to find the amount of something using numbers and math

measure find the size or amount of something

volume the amount that can be held in an object or shape

width the measurement of something from one side to the other

perimeter the line or edge that forms the outside of any shape

angle the space between two lines that come together at a single point

3-D (three-dimensional) having three dimensions: length, width, and depth; e.g., a sphere, cone, cylinder, pyramid, or prism

depth the distance from front to back or from top to bottom

pattern a repeated design

cylinder a shape with two ends that are circles and long straight sides

sphere a round shape, like a ball or a globe